KITCHEN FINANCIALS

The untold reality

THE UNTOLD REALITIES OF HOW TO CREATE AND MAINTAIN A PROFITABLE, PROFESSIONAL KITCHEN
VOLUME II

KITCHEN FINANCIALS

The untold reality

Tristan B. Jones

Copyright © 2020 by Tristan B. Jones

All rights reserved. No part of this publication may be reproduced, distributed, or transmitted in any form or by any means, including photocopying, recording, or other electronic or mechanical methods, without the prior written permission of the publisher, except in the case of brief quotations embodied in critical reviews and certain other noncommercial uses permitted by copyright law. For permission requests, write to the publisher, addressed "Attention: Permissions Coordinator," at the email below.

Chef.tristan.jones@gmail.com

Special thanks to Christopher Morris at Vice Design for the awesome cover art. You can reach him at

www.vicedesign.co

Contents

Preface 1

Intro... 3

Waste 6

Ordering 8

    Receiving 10

    Menu Creation 11

    Purveyors.. 20

    Broadliners 20

    Vegetables/Fruits................................... 24

    Dairy Guy 27

    Soft Drinks/Beverages........................... 29

    Miscellaneous 29

Yields 31

On the Line... 35

    Standardized recipes 35

    Portion control....................................... 36

    Sandbagging 40

Prep and how over kill costs 43

POS 45

Inventory 48

Food Cost/The Meat and Potatoes *51*
- Yield percentage 51
- Actual Product cost 52
- Plate components 53
- Cost per plate...54
- Basic food cost 55
- Extra Components.................................56
- Average food cost for your menu 59
- Actual Food Costs...................................61

Other Expenses *67*
- Paper 67
- Chemicals..69

Labor Cost *72*
- Hourly vs salary......................................75
- Cutting prep time 76
- My favorite system 79
- Menu balance 82

Profit Bombs *87*

In Summation *90*

Preface

I know when you are searching the internet for something to help you guide your food cost and other kitchen financial queries in the right direction, you have many options. Unfortunately, most of these options include things like textbooks filled with bullet points and pie charts. For many, not only is this tedious and boring, but it can be hard to retain the pertinent knowledge you paid for when buying the book.

I have learned how to work out and deal with kitchen financial issues in three ways. I attended culinary school, I have worked in numerous private restaurants as a chef dealing with accountants, and I have gone through the corporate world with all of their 'webinars'. After having held chef positions on three continents and dealing with a myriad of issues throughout my career, I thought I could distill what I have learned into a more pleasant reading/learning experience for those looking to manage their costs more professionally. Without the need for charts, graphs and redundant hyperbole.

Tristan B. Jones

Intro

Managing your kitchen financials is essential to any restaurant. Without the proper attention, you can very quickly run your own business into the ground. All of the math, technical terms, charts, graphs, and seemingly difficult aspects of managing your money in the kitchen can be intimidating. That's ok, it makes sense, most businesses are either retail, buying wholesale and selling the product to individuals, wholesale, buying even larger amounts and selling products to industrial, commercial, or institutional establishments, or manufacturers, who receive multiple products and turn them into a new product. In the kitchen, we are doing both retail and manufacturing in the same location. Hence, the math can be a little more complicated than selling a piece of equipment with a twenty percent markup. That's why I decided to condense my knowledge into an easy to read and more importantly, easy to understand book to help put the whole process into a painless, easy to digest package.

Food cost will take up a large portion of this book, as it is the easiest to misinterpret as well as the easiest to miss rectifiable problems that can lead to financial failure.

So what is food cost? Food cost, put simply, is how much money you spend on food. See, not too scary so far. In an average restaurant, around thirty percent of your budget is spent just making sure you have what you need in house to produce your menu. We are not discussing beverages or to-go boxes, we can touch on that later, but for now, we are just looking at food.

I'm assuming some of you out there are using the 'look inside' feature on Amazon looking for a quick and easy answer. Well, here it is.

If it costs you one dollar to produce a dish, and you sell it for ten dollars, you are at ten percent food cost.

Happy? That's the most basic way to put it. I bet you're thinking 'That sounds simple enough...' and it is. Is there more to the story? Of course, that's why I'm writing this book. I'm writing to help you understand

KITCHEN FINANCIALS

why such a simple calculation is not hard to master, but without ever having certain things brought to your attention, odds are your number will be so wildly inaccurate you are wasting your own time and as we all know, time is money.

Let's start by looking at what can kill your food cost before we get into the numbers, as well as some things you can do to squeeze every penny out of every service.

Tristan B. Jones

Waste

Waste is the antagonist of every culinary story. It covers a wide range of problems that encompass every aspect of the product in your kitchen. There are ways to mitigate the issues that cause waste, and these methods need to always be in the back of your mind.

What causes waste? There are a few factors. Someone could drop a perfectly good steak into bucket of soapy water. Food could sit in your walk in until it grows a green furry friend. You could have a careless cook that throws away a part of meat or vegetable that would have accounted for two more portions of a dish. Maybe someone left the salmon filets on the loading dock too long. All of these things can, but hopefully won't happen, so let's look at some of these possible follies.

We won't spend too much time discussing dropping or spilling food as there is not much you can do about that. I have seen restaurants that charge employees for mistakes, but this is a horrendous way to treat your staff. No one wants to work in an

KITCHEN FINANCIALS

establishment where accidents have financial consequences.

    Food sitting in your walk in for too long is huge problem throughout the industry. You need to utilize all products before it's too late. Generally when something sits too long, it is because of an issue with ordering, so let's look at how you can ensure this doesn't happen to you.

Ordering

All of the food you bring into your restaurant begins with an order. Making ordering mistakes is the first place you can fail when trying to manage costs to ensure profitability. Over ordering will lead to spoilage and under ordering will lead to 86ing items, which will lose customers. Either way, your bottom line is what's taking the hit.

Your first line of defense when ordering food is establishing par levels. So what are par levels? Your par level is how many of each dish or product you need for a day, or until you can receive another order. Generally, your par changes depending on the day as some days of the week will be busier than others. This can be done mathematically, or by the gut feeling of the chef.

In business, we all like everything to be done precisely. Unfortunately, with par levels you can start with such a number, but the person doing the ordering will get a good sense of fluctuations quickly. You might

KITCHEN FINANCIALS

normally sell twenty bowls of French onion soup and ten bowls of vichyssoise, but when a warm front moves in those numbers can reverse. The manager in charge of ordering should be able to track and manage these fluctuations.

With proper par levels in place, you can feel confident that when you place an order, you won't be receiving too much or not enough. It is a step that can seriously reduce the amount of stress you have to deal with on a day to day basis. At the same time, you will not have to worry about an extra twenty pounds of beef going bad in your walk in.

Some owners/managers tend to have the common mindset of thinking they should go to a grocery store for items of which they only need a small amount. This is a mistake as now you are not only paying retail, but you have a lot more receipts to keep up with. So either you or your accountant will end up spending more time consolidating the information. Time is money in any business, and the extra time can end up leading to drastic mistakes causing financial audits.

Receiving

Properly receiving goods is important to ensure both compliance and quality. Making mistakes such as leaving food unattended on a loading dock or putting an item that should be frozen in the fridge will damage the quality and shelf life of the product. This seems obvious, and it is, but you have to remember, no one person will be doing all of the receiving. You need to properly train all staff members to do so, or your food cost can suffer as well as wasting a lot more product than is absolutely necessary.

The biggest issue with receiving is timing. Most kitchens want their order to arrive when there staff does in the morning. The issue is, a lot of kitchens all fight for the same delivery time, say seven in the morning, and this is a huge problem for distributors. Usually, the distributor will favor the largest and most profitable account as they want to keep their big fish happy. With such a large volume of restaurants in any given city, this causes scheduling issues.

KITCHEN FINANCIALS

Furthermore, a lot of places have their cooks come in at seven am and set up the food delivery at the same time. This is not what you want to do. Your delivery guy might be ten minutes early and your staff ten minutes late. The average delivery man will not wait around for twenty minutes. You end up having to wait until the afternoon for your food, causing not only the issue of 86ing menu items, but also sometimes they show up during dinner or lunch rush, causing your line to crash and burn.

The ideal delivery time in the morning is thirty minutes after your staff arrives, this solves the timing issue for both parties and gives the people in your kitchen time to get their whites on and to get the kitchen up and running.

Menu Creation

Creating a good menu is much more than putting good dish ideas on a piece of paper. One of the most important things to consider is, 'where else will this menu item be used?'

How you build your menu drastically affects your food cost in many ways. It influences multiple aspects of the kitchen as they pertain to food cost such as; the amount of product on hand at any given time or par, the number of products kept in house, the rate at which the product is used, the amount of money needed to purchase a product based on desired quality, as well as the price point available at that time.

Let's look at these factors and see how we can mitigate some potential losses.

'The amount of product on hand at any given time, or par'. The less of an item you need, generally, the more waste there is. It seems counterintuitive, as one would think if you order a small amount of something it will be easy to use quickly. The problem is there are very few items from any large supplier of which you can actually receive small amounts. A lot of suppliers have what they call 'split cases', where you can for example take one jar of capers rather than a whole case, but this is not always the case. Having already discussed the evils of going to a grocery store, we will move on.

'The number of products kept in house.' It is of upmost importance to keep what you have in house to an absolute minimum. People tend to forget that every

KITCHEN FINANCIALS

item sitting on your shelf is money. There is no food sitting on the shelf, it's all money. The more you have sitting on the shelf, the more you are 'in the hole' as they say. We will do some quick math to see what I mean.

If you have fifteen menu items with five components each, that is seventy five items. Let's say you use onions on five dishes, that is now seventy four items. Fifteen items is a very small menu. If you increase the menu size to what an average chain restaurant in America is, for example you are looking at thirty five menu items. You can start to see how the amount of stock in house can quickly spin out of control.

The easiest way to keep this in check is to utilize as many products in as many dishes as possible. So when designing a menu, if you have mozzarella for your baked ziti, rather than ordering shredded for it, maybe order it as a brick and do mozzarella sticks as well. This can eat into your labor cost, but we will discuss that later.

'The rate at which product is used.' Some ingredients have longer shelf lives than others. We all know this, but if it is not taken into consideration when building your menu, your bottom line will suffer.

If you make a menu with a large amount of food that perishes quickly, your waste percentage grows drastically. Things like bananas, avocados, and peaches, should not be a large percentage of the necessary ingredients. You will have some, of course, but the less you can use the better chance you have of saving money. Try to use ingredients that last, such as potatoes and butternut squash or pumpkin. Some ingredients can last an extremely long time such as canned goods and dried pasta, and are a very thrifty way to save money.

The amount of fresh vs frozen or dried will depend on your style of restaurant. I am not suggesting you should serve canned green beans to anyone, ever. I'm simply saying that if you want to make a menu item with a highly perishable ingredient you might want to consider an option in which the ingredient is preserved in some way. A good example is pasta with truffle. There are some good products out there that are manufactured with fresh truffles, and they have a wonderful flavor as well as an excellent shelf life. Just make sure the rate

KITCHEN FINANCIALS

of which the product is used is comparable with the amount you can order in at a time, or suffer the consequences.

'The amount of money needed to purchase a product based on desired quality.' As I just said, make sure the quality of your food doesn't suffer. However there are many money saving options out there that can help keep costs down without directly effecting quality. For example, if you have an eight ounce chicken breast with butternut squash puree and honey glazed parsnips as a main and chicken caesar salad as a salad option, can you save money on chicken? Of course you can.

In this instance, most owners/kitchen managers will simply order in eight ounce breasts, cook them on the grill, and slice the ones for the salad to order. I'm not saying this system is evil, but you do have alternatives. Purveyors generally have what they call 'random' cuts. They range in size so you have to find the ones that are right for you, but they are viable options. Usually, they are listed as eight ounce random, ten ounce random etc. You might think the eight ounce random is the way to go in this instance, but you are going to want to get ten or larger.

The way it works is the number given is the average size of the largest pieces. So if you order eight, ninety percent of the box might come in smaller than eight ounces, meaning they are not viable to use on your main. So be careful. The financial upside is worth considering however. If you normally pay two dollars and ninety four cents per pound, but you can get the random cut for one dollar ninety seven, you can save a lot of money long term.

Another issue to consider is buying a lower quality product without it affecting your final dish. A good example would be a foie gras pate. Foie is generally graded with either A,B, or C, all pertaining to the quality. I would never suggest C for anything, but the difference between A and B will be negligible once pureed and chilled. Financially however, you will save a lot of money.

I would like to say, I would never want anyone to serve an inferior product as this will lead to unsatisfied customers. I would just like to point out that there are cheaper alternatives to a lot of products in the

KITCHEN FINANCIALS

kitchen. Having a good chef go over options and doing test runs on any item you wish to save money on is very important. Don't end up angering your customers and ruining your own business by trying to save money, but don't be afraid to explore alternatives.

'What is the price point available at any given time'? With modern food trends, many people like to get wrapped up in things such as seasonal ingredients and farm to table practices. The funny thing is, this has always been around, and it never went away. In America, it was almost completely destroyed, but in other parts of the world there is no phrase to describe these practices. They are simply how things are, and always have been done. When it comes to saving you money, these practices can be beneficial, or not.

The rule of thumb here is always to cook what is in season. This is in fine dining establishments with seasonal menus, but you can still take advantage of seasons even in something as far down the scale as a diner. If you own a diner, there are many items you must have regardless of the season.

Tristan B. Jones

I am an American, and if I walk into a diner without a burger on the menu I might have a heart attack out of sheer confusion. On that burger, you need lettuce and tomato right? Well it's January, so it's definitely not in season. In cases like this, it is understandable that you have to pay for that lettuce to be shipped from Peru, hence increasing the cost. But that doesn't mean you can't take advantage of seasons.

For any menu, it is good to have some flexibility. For some it is a daily or weekly special, for others it could be just a soup. Some places even write over half of their menus on chalk boards every day just to ebb and flow with the market and product in house. All of these are reasonable, and take advantage of what is cheap based on seasonality. When a fruit or vegetable gets into local harvest time, the prices drop dramatically. That's why it is good practice to check local farmers markets and such for this drop. Don't be afraid to ask some farmers when the main squash harvest will be in full swing. They will have an abundant amount to sell as will other farmers. This leads to them having to drop the price to stay competitive.

KITCHEN FINANCIALS

I know what some might be thinking, 'That sounds like a predatory business practice to me.' But it's not. The fruits and vegetables are ripe when they are ripe. You can't help that. Do you think a farmer would rather sell you a green unripe orange for twice the price two months early? No, they want to prove that their product is quality just as you do and for the same reasons you do. It's all about repeat business, and selling all products at the right time ensures quality and minimum waste.

When working on a menu, the most important thing to remember is to do it with someone who knows how all of this works. After reading this, you might feel you are equipped to do so by yourself, and hey, maybe you are, that's why I'm writing this, to help you out. But I would still suggest at the bare minimum *consulting* a professional chef. The rates will vary from chef to chef, but like tattoos, good ones aren't cheap and cheapo ones aren't good. Keep that in mind. This leads me to my next point, where you should be purchasing your food.

Tristan B. Jones

Purveyors

As I said, keeping things local and in season can help, but beyond that, where should you get your food? Once again, this is not a simple answer, I would love to give you a name of a company and send you on your way, but this is the worst way to set up your restaurant. Generally, for any restaurant, you have what we call a broadliner, a veg guy, a dairy guy, sometimes a soft drink guy, (depending on if the back of the house orders drinks, juices etc.), and one or more smaller miscellaneous vendors for things you may not be able to get from the aforementioned purveyors.

I know it can seem complicated, but it really isn't, and this system can drastically help you control your costs long term. So let's look at these purveyors and what to look for when deciding who to use, or who to switch to.

Broadliners

Your broadliner is a large food service company that will provide anywhere from fifty to eighty percent of your total food purchases. Some will even give you

KITCHEN FINANCIALS

discounts for using their company for certain percentage of your total purchases. There not a large amount out there that you can use based on where you are located, so you might be stuck with what's available. Some larger markets however, will have three or four options. So how do you choose?

When contacting these companies for the first time, they will ask the basic questions such as your name, restaurant name, and address. This will allow them to get you in their system so they can see who your representative will be, or if in fact, they even deliver to your area. Once in the system you will be provided with, among other things, your account number and credentials needed to log in to their online ordering platform. If you feel more comfortable with a face to face, you can request a meeting with the representative for your area, but this is largely unnecessary as to start, you simply want to see what they offer. Also, if you do decide to do business with their company, the representative will come visit you and get the handshake part of business taken care of.

Once on their online ordering platform, you can get an idea of what they offer. I suggest printing out your menu with ingredients and enough space to take notes. If you would like a vermicelli dish on your menu and they don't have it or it is a 'back order' item, this could potentially cause a lot of headache down the line.

What is a back order item you ask? Well this is a broad term, as each company has a different name for it. Some say 'select item', or 'international item', and many other names, but they all mean the same thing. You can't just order it as you normally would. Some can take a week to arrive and others a month. I think it goes without explanation that this kind of latency in an order can crash your business. Rule number one of catering if you have it as a service is you can do pretty much anything. I say pretty much as a fine dining establishment can do more than a diner, however if you tell someone you can, but you didn't realize you couldn't get a product, you lose a customer and your reputation.

Sometimes, you need to think about availability in the future as well. If you plan on making Christmas goose like your grandmother did when Christmas comes around, make sure you look into that. I suggest looking into different proteins early and extensively if there is even a chance you might want to have it on your menu.

You also need check available delivery times and dates that are available. If you don't see something you like on the website, don't immediately decide they are not right for you. A lot of scheduling issues can be fixed with a quick conversation with your representative.

Next, you need to check the quality of the products offered. If you would like to open a steakhouse for instance, your broadliner is not going to be your best bet most of the time. In many countries, the quality of beef available might not be what you are looking for. I have seen broadliners that only sell choice and select beef for example, with maybe one or two exceptions. If they do have a product but you would like to test it out yourself, never be afraid to ask for a sample.

For most broadliners, you can speak with your representative and get samples. Their company knows that if you are going to choose them they will have millions of dollars of business from you over the coming years, so a few steaks won't scare them. I do however suggest you have a complete list of the products you would like to try before you ask your representative. Some of these items will involve your rep going to a warehouse and personally splitting a case. This is a huge inconvenience and it is often done at the personal expense of your rep. Treat him/her right, and he/she should treat you right in turn.

Your broadliner will be providing most of your proteins and dry goods, so these are the areas that need the most attention. For the rest of your products, it is generally advantageous to go with another company.

Vegetables/Fruits

Although your broadliner is essential, when it comes to vegetables they more often than not don't meet your needs as a restaurant. The biggest issue is generally the quality of the product and the availability.

With so many restaurants using the same broadliner for absolutely everything, they go through millions of pounds of veg a week depending on the country, and size of

KITCHEN FINANCIALS

the company. (But remember you can get most things because of their size.) This leads to problems in the quality of their product. It doesn't matter how big of a company you are or how many employees you have, you can't verify every piece of veg as being ripe. All you can do when moving massive amounts of products is try to extend the shelf life as much as possible. This leads to things like gassing tomatoes to turn them red. This practice is why most commercial tomatoes you buy have no flavor, you are essentially eating a tomato that is green, but has been gassed to ensure a red color. Their company is as worried about waste as you are, so they cut corners.

This is why it is imperative you find a quality vegetable purveyor. I should mention here, 'veg guy' is just a term used in restaurants; the purveyor will generally have fruits, vegetables, and other assorted products, but fruits and vegetables are why you have his number. Most cities have a vegetable company that is there to fix the problems of the larger companies. Some started out as a vegetable purveyor before the world turned into what it is now, and the business just slowly evolved into something that can stay competitive in the modern market.

You need to ask your potential vendor questions specifically focused on the quality of his products. If you want good tomatoes, ask him if his company gasses them. Ask him if you can order bananas in different stages of ripeness. (You usually can, you can order ripe or green.) Find out where his product comes from. If he tells you it is all local, ask about getting lettuce in the winter. If he doesn't mention massive greenhouses, he's probably just lying to get your business. Obviously no one is growing durian in Chicago, but find out about the products you will be using the most. If all of his tomatoes come from another country for example, you will take a hit on costs as you now have to help pay the import tax. You might however, save money because the labor cost to harvest is cheaper in another country.

Basically, your vegetable guy will be just that, your vegetable guy. Having one vendor to handle one specific set of products can greatly increase the quality you receive, leading to happier customers and repeat business.

KITCHEN FINANCIALS

Dairy Guy

The days of the milk man delivering to your door has long been replaced with plastic jugs at the supermarket, but the idea lives on in restaurants. With dairy, you run into a similar issue of shelf life as you did with veg when it comes to your broadliner. Not only are they trying to make things last longer, but they also need to move massive amounts of products that perish quickly

Do you need a dairy guy? No, that's the short answer. If your restaurant doesn't use much milk and cream, odds are you don't need one. Even if this is the case, I do still suggest looking into it.

Your dairy guy is helpful for numerous reasons, but first let's looks at shelf life. Odds are, if you order a gallon of milk from a broadliner, it has been on a long journey. You may live in Texas, but your milk is from Wisconsin. The cow has to be milked, that milk is pasteurized, packaged, and shipped to a warehouse and waits. From there, the large distribution hub that is in your area orders eight hundred gallons, which is then shipped across state lines again, and then another wait. Finally you order it; it gets loaded, and comes to you. The logistics of this system have been worked out so that you as a customer receive a reasonable product, but is it worth it?

Well, it can be. Odds are you don't want a whole new vendor if you only use one gallon of milk a week, but most restaurants use significantly more than that. With a local dairy guy, you can work with a company that uses farms nearby that all come together in one warehouse in one area, cutting out one of the middle men. The product you receive will normally have a longer shelf life, therefore producing less waste. If you pay three dollars from a broadliner with five days before it goes bad, or three dollars and twenty-five cents locally and it lasts a week and a half, which choice will ultimately help your bottom line? It depends on the business and the volume of product used as well as the availability of delivery times, but it is something to consider.

Along with perishability, many dairy guys will have an assortment of cheeses you won't be able to find anywhere else. Let's be honest, most goat cheeses in America are sub-par. Many times, you can't even find a cheese close to what you are looking for.

KITCHEN FINANCIALS

Your dairy guy on the other hand, might have a line of cheeses from a local farmer that happens to be making some amazing products.

Soft Drinks/Beverages

Your front of the house might take care of this, but it depends on how your establishment is set up. Generally speaking, beverage cost is not part of your food cost. If it is, I would suggest changing the system as this can make it hard to be accurate when deciphering your P&L statements. (Profit/loss statements.) As this book is geared towards kitchen financials I will move on, but I do seriously suggest not having it attached to your food cost.

Miscellaneous

Odds are there is something you want on your menu that you can't get from any of the aforementioned purveyors, and that's ok. A lot of restaurants go outside their main vendors for this reason. It could be a rabbit special, or a vendor that only deals in truffles. There is no reason to worry about using vendors outside of the norm. These also include trips to the grocery store for something might need quickly.

Tristan B. Jones

The biggest mistake I've seen as a consultant is restaurants not properly cataloguing these purchases. Make sure you have a system in place and a special row in your spreadsheet to account for these purchases. I have seen too many places asking why their numbers don't add up as someone walks in the door with a bag from their local supermarket. So pay attention.

KITCHEN FINANCIALS

Yields

Yield percentages are another common mistake I've seen in my time as a chef/consultant. I have seen too many people design their own spreadsheet and not take this number into account. So what is a yield percentage?

Your yield percentage is the amount of food wasted after preparing an item for service. Let's say you have a beef tenderloin that you order in whole. It weighs ten pounds and you want it in one pound portions. I've seen a lot of people say, 'Ok, so we should get ten portions.' But this is not the case. First off, when it comes in it needs to be trimmed. You need to take all of the silver skin and extra fat off of it right? So how much did you lose in the process? That is your yield percentage number. If you trim .3 pounds off of it, you are now left with a ninety-seven percent yield, or if you took one pound off, you have a ninety percent yield. This means you have less than ten portions. What about the small end of the tenderloin? Usually that would be cut off, adding to your waste.

Tristan B. Jones

This is a common mistake people make, as it pertains to almost every item that must be processed in house. Even things like zucchini and squash have yield percentages. You don't eat the hard knob at the top do you? No, but you do pay for it just the same as you pay for the rest of it. So how then, do you deal with the problem without going crazy? I've seen a few different methods.

I have worked in places that kept buckets for waste. Some have one for meat and one for veg. The idea behind this is you can weigh it and see how much you are losing. Personally, I think this is a ridiculous system. You end up with a stinky disgusting bucket next to you all day waiting for a health inspector to make a negative mark on his score sheet. Beyond that, it is wildly inaccurate. You generally see this practice in large corporations. These methods are generally being developed by people who have no idea how a kitchens actually work. The system was designed by people who have as much business deciding how kitchens should work as I do performing heart surgery.

KITCHEN FINANCIALS

The best system, my system generally, is to find out the percentages for each item and get it out of the way. It is actually simple to do.

You order in your product, process it to a servable level, and see what's left. It's that easy. If you start with ten pounds of carrots and you end up with nine point five pounds, you have a ninety five percent yield. There really is no magic or complicated mathematics behind it, regardless of what that food cost text book you bought tells you. You also have to remember, if you use those carrot peelings to make a stock, you didn't technically waste anything. You do however still need to know the percentage number so you can calculate what you need to order.

With small groups or events, it is pretty easy to know what you need, but if you want to cater for a thousand people, not knowing your yield percentage can have you over or under ordering food, leading to disaster. That's why I recommend knowing your yields for most, if not all products you use.

Most professional chefs know these basic percentages by heart. How much waste comes off a brisket for smoking or what the yield is for a whole carrot has been seen so many times its burned into their memories. Obviously no one person can have all of these numbers for every ingredient in the world memorized, but a quick consultation call might save you some time and effort.

KITCHEN FINANCIALS

On the Line

Standardized recipes

Standardized recipes will save you a lot of headache. They are the heart of the products you would like to be proud of when you serve them to the masses. Just because a cook has experience, doesn't mean he knows how you want things done in your restaurant. There is an old saying that goes, 'how many cooks does it take to change a light bulb? Eight, one to change the bulb and seven to tell you how they did it in their old kitchen.' Its cliché at this point, but still very true.

A notebook or binder with standardized recipes will not only ensure consistency of product, but cost per plate as well. It is impossible to properly track food costs when cook A is using six ounces of meat, cook B is using eight ounces of meat, and cook C is using ten ounces of meat. How about how many pounds of onions do you use to make thirty portions of goulash? The more consistent you can be, the better it is for you, as well as your customers.

To create a standardized recipe notebook, you will need a chef. This is not to say you will need to hire a full time chef if you are slinging sandwiches from a food cart, but I would suggest finding a good one and hiring him hourly as a consultant, to help with such matters.

Portion control

Portion control is very important for food cost in the same way as standardized recipes, it's just slightly different. The numbers for portion control are generally in your standardized recipes; however standardized recipes are not always related to portion control. Sound confusing? It's not, I promise.

Let's say you serve shrimp stir fry. You have shrimp, vegetables, and a sauce for flavor. Your standardized recipe will tell you how to make that sauce. Two ounces of soy sauce, four ounces of oyster sauce, and one ounce of mirin, for example. The recipe might go on to say how many ounces of

KITCHEN FINANCIALS

shrimp go on a plate as well, most do, but some don't. Portion control is the amount of shrimp or snow peas on a given plate. It could be by weight, or by count, depending on the situation, restaurant, and ingredient.

If you own a kitchen and don't own at least one scale, the odds of you closing your doors are very high. You need to have the same amount of product on each plate. How many times have you and your wife both ordered shrimp stir fry from your local Chinese joint, and when it arrives, you have ten shrimp and your wife gets two? Obviously in this instance it is because they were cooked at the same time in the same wok, but the end result is the same as if you ordered them on separate occasions. The customer will still be unhappy.

How do you portion control everything in your restaurant? Luckily, this problem has been around for a very long time, so you don't have to re-invent the wheel. To start, you need to weigh everything you can for your recipes. Liquids are easier by volume unless you are baking, but weight is important. You need to know exactly how many grams/ounces of meat you have on your sandwich. No one likes a Philly full of beef one day and half full the next. For liquids at service, such as the cheese sauce on a Philly, the right size ladle is the easiest way to go. All commercial ladles have the ounces and/or milliliters on the handle, the most common for sauces being a two ounce.

One of the biggest killers I've seen when it comes to portion control is how small side dishes like fries are handled. How much does a single fry cost? Well, not much, definitely less than one cent depending on cut and manufacturer. For our purposes, let's use a cool one cent. Anyone out there reading this that has ever seen a kitchen operate that sells fries knows that a lot of the time, there are fries left over in the kitchen after plating. It may be only four or five fries, but that's four or five cents.

If you serve fifty portions of fries and you lose five cents every time you serve a portion, that is two dollars and fifty cents. Multiply that times three hundred and sixty-five days, you get nine hundred and twelve dollars and fifty cents. That is almost a thousand dollars a year or seventy-six dollars a month on one single item. It may not sound like much to you, but what if you do three types of fries, onion rings, and your

KITCHEN FINANCIALS

sauces aren't measured etc. All of this adds up to hundreds or thousands of dollars a month.

Now I realize, most restaurants and chefs do no weigh their fries. Some will use some kind of cup measuring tool, but it is still inaccurate. So why is everyone not weighing fries? Well it comes down to labor costs. If you do lose two dollars and fifty cents a day on fries, can your worker weigh portions of fries fast enough to save that money or will you be dumping that cost right back into labor.

For kitchens that experience slower times and are nice and tidy, weighing things like fries can be advantageous. For larger busier operations, it probably is not. It is up to you as the person in charge of food cost to make the decision of whether or not implementing a system like this is worth it in your restaurant.

Utilizing standardized recipes along with portion control will create a situation in which it is possible to track the pertinent costs. Without them you will have wild fluctuations in your numbers and will have an extremely difficult time keeping yourself sane.

Sandbagging

Sandbagging is another kitchen term that is used ubiquitously throughout kitchens, and does in fact happen in almost every kitchen. This is another one that effects lower end kitchen more than their upscale brothers, but it does happen almost everywhere. So what is it hand how does it pertain to food cost?

Essentially, sandbagging is the practice of preparing something that before an order comes in for it. This only pertains to items that cannot be re-used if it does not get sold, otherwise we would be talking about prep. I would like to make it very clear that sandbagging is not always evil. Depending on your establishment and its normal amounts of a certain dish sold, it can actually increase customer satisfaction and create greater diner turnover rates leading to higher profits. In some cases, however, it does the opposite. Let's look at the good and the bad.

KITCHEN FINANCIALS

The reason sandbagging is frowned upon in most restaurant is the diminished quality of a product after it has been sitting around waiting on an order. This rings true for fried items and things that can become over-cooked or dried out. Once an item has been sitting too long, it must be dumped to ensure you are still selling a quality product to your customer. This of course, kills your cost. If you have a cook constantly making two burgers when he has an order for one just to make his life easier, you will end up throwing away a lot of dead cow. I have seen this food cost killer taking place in more restaurants than I care to mention.

The good aspects can help your customer satisfaction, but generally not your food cost. Let's say your restaurant serves a lasagna that takes seventeen minutes to heat up when pulled from the fridge. If you sell a minimum of twenty lasagnas every Friday without fail, it wouldn't hurt to pull some portions out of the fridge to start warming up after each one or two sold. This can reduce ticket times leading to greater customer satisfaction and repeat business.

The point is, sandbagging is not necessarily a bad thing, but allowing it to happen in your kitchen without oversight can kill your food cost, and hence your business. Make sure you pay attention to who is sandbagging what, and why.

KITCHEN FINANCIALS

Prep and how over kill costs

Many of the products you prepare for service lose a great deal of shelf life once you process them into your mise en place for a station. A couple quick examples to illustrate my point quickly would be avocados processed into guacamole or eggs, separated and turned into hollandaise. An egg can last two weeks in the shell, the hollandaise dies quickly. And I think we have all been to a friend's house for a party with a giant bowl of black guacamole. The amount of food you prep can kill your food cost as much as anything else I've mentioned in this book. You need to control how much is prepped, but more importantly why.

Previously, I had discussed par levels as they pertain to ordering. Your mise en place work on a similar par system. You need to know how many portions of any given item you need to prepare for service. This is impossible without having a track record, so for new restaurants you just have to make sure you don't run out, and follow your numbers day by day.

Tristan B. Jones

Any cook who has been in any restaurant at any station for a few months knows what his/her par levels are by heart. Walk into any restaurants kitchen, look at a cook's mise en place, and ask. "Do you have enough of this for today?" I guarantee he/she will have an answer. This is because after months or years of working in that restaurant he/she knows about how much of any given item he/she will need. The cook will know running out is not an option, therefore if more needs to be prepped, he/she should get moving.

It is a balance. If you under prep, you will run out of something and have to eighty-six an item. If you over prep, you end up throwing food away, killing your costs. Your cooks on the line and your POS machine are invaluable tools you must use to ensure the right amount of prep is done so you don't kill your costs. So what is a POS anyway?

KITCHEN FINANCIALS

POS

Ah yes, the Point of Sales system, this is an integral part of any kitchen in the modern world. Is it a necessary evil? No, but the headaches it will save you in the long run are almost are countless. Your POS will help you with all aspects of your business, but as we are focusing on the kitchen, we will stay focused.

Your point of sales system can be an integral part of controlling your operational costs. I say it can be, because it is not entirely necessary, however I do recommend it. Your POS will allow you to track every dime of your food sales down to a T. When it comes to tracking how much food is sold and what kind of food is sold, it is an invaluable tool.

You can of course forego the cost of such a system but if you do choose to take this route, you will have to track all sales and outgoing food by hand using the tickets brought into the kitchen. This might sound like a viable option once you see the price tag on some of the systems, but trust me when I say, it isn't.

Along with helping cooks during service and with inventory, the POS can help with food walking out of the kitchen in someone's backpack as well. If you order fifty steaks and you look at the end of the night and you have ten, did you sell that many or is someone feeding their family? A quick jog over to the POS station will clear that right up. You can select any dish and see how many were sold that night. If you only sold thirty, you might want to have a chat with your staff.

Aside from what I have mentioned here, POS systems can have a wide range of uses. Which company you choose to do business with will decide which options you will have. It's kind of like buying a car; you can get the fully loaded or the base model. I would suggest shopping around in your area and doing your due diligence rather than settling on the first company to walk through your door. If you read this and decide to get yourself a POS system and you do have issues with it at some point, and you will, just remember I did sum up by warning you with this. The acronym POS has a different

KITCHEN FINANCIALS

set of affiliated words for veterans of the industry, so please don't email me complaining you are having problems, contact the company you chose, and have fun.

Tristan B. Jones

Inventory

Keeping a proper inventory is an extremely important aspect of controlling food costs. You need to know what product is in your kitchen at all times. There are so many mistakes that can be made by management that doesn't know what is already on the shelf.

When ordering food, you can't know what is needed without knowing what you already have. If you have twenty pounds of cheese, but you can't remember if it is still there or if you did in fact order it last week, so you order it anyway, odds are that product will be moldy before it gets used. As the person controlling food cost, you should know everything you have on hand at all times anyway, but regimented inventory cycles are still crucial. That being said, there is more than one way to go about it.

One of the most common ways of doing inventory is having the staff do it. For me, this is the worst possible way to get it done. Let me explain. For starters, your staff is busy. If they are not busy with service or

KITCHEN FINANCIALS

prep, they are cleaning. Most places that integrate the staff driven inventory policy justify if by saying, 'One station does dry storage, one does walk in etc., so there really isn't that much extra work...' Although this might be true, you are still taking valuable time away from your staff whose time is much better utilized performing the aforementioned tasks.

In addition, you will end up with different counts for the same inventory. One staff member might see a bag and a half of fusilli; another might see 1.3 bags of the same product. It doesn't seem like much, but if this continues throughout the whole process, you could end up with thousands of dollars difference in the numbers, depending on the size and scale of your establishment. Inventory should be done by management, and management only in my opinion.

That being said, how and when the task is performed by management matters as well. Do you have a spreadsheet prepared? You should. If you try to do inventory free hand you will end up spending hours sifting through hand written scribbles trying to decipher their meaning. Even if the entire sheet is legible, you still have to calculate the total amount of money sitting on the shelf. Will you thumb through invoices for hours on end, or do the equivalent on a website's ordering page? I hope not, do yourself a favor, and either create a spreadsheet or use a POS, (point of sales), system with an integrated inventory platform. This will not only be more concise and consistent, but it will help keep you sane.

KITCHEN FINANCIALS

Food Cost/The Meat and Potatoes

So let's get down to it. I wanted you to understand what the general aspects of controlling food costs were, before boring you with mathematics. I will still keep it simple and easy to understand, as that was the point of me writing this, but there will have to be some obligatory equations in here.

Yield percentage

As I mentioned before, yield percentage is very important. Once you have your yield percentage, you can calculate the *actual* cost of your product. This is what you are actually paying for the usable product after processing. So let's have a look at the numbers, shall we?

The formula for Actual Product Cost goes like this:

You start with what your Usable Product *after* processing:

Ordered Weight (OW): 1lb
Waste Weight (WW): 0.1
(OW) 1 − (WW) .01 = 0.9 (UP) Usable Product

Yield Percentage formula is:

(UP) 0.9 / (OW) 1 = .9 x 100 = 90 Yield Percentage

So basically, you are simply finding out what the percentage of the ordered product is waste. Remember, you only need to calculate your yield percentage from a given product once, after that, you only need this.

Actual Product cost

Now, you can calculate the number you really need, Actual Cost:
Original Cost (OC) = $15.00
Yield Percentage (YP) = 90%
100 / 90 = 1.1111
(OC) 15.00 x 1.1111 = $16.67 (APC) Actual Product Cost

So when you purchase a product, this is how you can find how much you are

KITCHEN FINANCIALS

actually paying for usable product, or your *Actual Cost.*

When calculating your food cost, it is important to use your actual cost, not what you are paying on your order sheet, as they are different numbers, and they don't lean in your favor.

Plate components

Each component of a plate has its own inherent cost. This is where standardized recipes and portion control shine. Let's say you have a dish that contains a steak with cognac cream sauce, steamed carrots, and a baked potato. We know the cost of the steak, potato, and carrots, but you make your sauce in bulk, so you start with your recipe.

The recipe makes ten ounces. You have ten ounces of cream, one ounce of cognac, salt and pepper. Let's say you use two ounces of sauce for each dish.

Your recipe shows:
10 oz cream : $6.00
1 oz cognac : $4.00

This means all ingredients combined is:

6.00 + 4.00 = $10.00

Total Cost : $10.00

To find the cost per portion you simply divide the total cost by the amount of servings you will get from the recipe:

Total Cost (TC) : $10.00
Amount of Servings per recipe (AS) : 5

10 (TC) / 5 (AS) = 2

Cost Per Serving (CPS) = $2.00

So it cost two dollars per portion for this component. Notice I did not factor in salt and pepper nor did I include loss in production. More on that later, for now, we are keeping it simple.

Cost per plate

Knowing your cost per plate is essential for knowing what your food cost percentage is. You cannot know at what

KITCHEN FINANCIALS

percentage your menu items are being sold without this number. Your cost per plate is the sum of all the components of a dish added together. We will continue using the steak dish as an example.

>   Steak (S) = $5.00
>   Carrots (C) = $2.00
>   Potato (P) = $1.00
>   Sauce (SA) = $2.00
>
>   So it's:
>
>   5 (S) + 2 (C) + 1 (P) + 2 (SA) = 10
>
>   Cost Per Plate (CPP) = $10.00

Basic food cost

Your basic food cost percentage is what it costs to produce a plate of food, divided by what you sell the food for, times one hundred to make it a percentage. So it is simply:

>   Selling Price (SP) = $20.00
>   Cost Per Plate (CPP) = $10.00
>   10 (CPP) / 20 (SP) = .5
>   .5 x 100 = 50

So its 50% Food Cost Percentage (FCP)

This is basic food cost. This does not take into account yield, or any other factors such as labor. I know many successful restaurants that use this simple calculation and are very successful as a business and add other costs such as labor and waste as another calculation. Some do not deal with yield at all, but that is a slippery slope. To factor in the yield, simply use your Actual Product Costs for all the components.

Extra Components

This basic calculation might leave you wondering about the other food products involved that were not mentioned i.e. salt, spices, and oils used for cooking. This can be accounted for in two ways; either by adding a percentage of the Cost Per Plate, or as a simple addition of a set cost. Different chefs in different kitchens do whichever way they feel more comfortable with, or, depending on the types of food and what goes into them.

If you run a burger joint, simply adding on a small amount at the end of a Cost Per Plate might be fine. Generally, you

KITCHEN FINANCIALS

will be using salt, and maybe a small amount of other spices and seasonings. Adding a few cents to your Cost Per Plate will cover such expenses. I usually add between three and five cents per.

So it would be:

Cost Per Plate (CPP) = $10.00
Seasoning Standard (SS) = $0.04

10.00 (CPP) + 0.04 (SS) = 10.04

So your actual cost for this plate is $10.04

To add this in as a percentage, it would be:

Cost Per Plate (CPP) = $10.00
Percent Added (PA) = 5%

5 (PA) / 100 = 0.05
.05 x 10 (CPP) = .5
10 (CPP) + .5 = 10.5

So your actual Cost for this plate is $10.50

Which method you choose is up to you. The main thing to remember is if it is a large enough expense, you need to factor it into food cost as an ingredient. If your spices and seasonings are extensive and expensive, you will either have to add a larger percent or sum to your Cost Per Plate. Some cuisines such as Indian food use many different spices, some of which are very expensive in each dish. So this definitely needs to be considered.

I know that trying to figure out what .002 ounces of turmeric costs sounds like it will drive you crazy and it can. That is why you implement one of these two methods. Not only is it extremely tedious to work out prices on such small amounts, it is generally inaccurate, as you cannot weigh each item as it goes into a sauté pan during service. So if you think you might be pinching pennies trying to work out the cost of the salt you are seasoning a steak with or how much oil goes into a pan before searing something, you are just wasting your time.

KITCHEN FINANCIALS

Average food cost for your menu

Your average food cost is the number that describes what percentage your entire menu averages out to. If one dish is at ten percent and one is at twenty, then your average is fifteen percent. You need to know your average as this number is what matters the most. Figuring it out is simple, and works like finding any other average.

It goes like this:

Food Cost Percentage of Individual Dishes (IDP)#1 (IDP)#2 (IDP)#3 (IDP)#4 and so on, all added together, then divided by the number of dishes added.
So:

(IDP) #1 + (IDP) #2 + (IDP) #3 + (IDP) #4 = X
X / 4 = Average Food cost

With numbers, it would look like this:

20 + 18 + 24 + 32 = 94
94 / 4 = 23.5

Tristan B. Jones

So your average food cost for your menu is 23.5%.

KITCHEN FINANCIALS

Actual Food Costs

I will preface this with a disclaimer. I have a friend that is an accountant, as some of you may know. He thinks this is ridiculous. I must say, I don't fully disagree. However, one of the largest food service companies in the world uses this system. So regardless of what you think of the system, I included it so you know how the big boys play.

I bet at this point you think we are finished with the calculations, and we very well could be. Most restaurants in the world operate using the food cost calculations above. Unfortunately, there is more to the story.

Remember all that talk about inventory? Well it wasn't just for laughs. You have to take what we call *Managed Volume* into account. You see, as I said before, everything sitting on your shelf costs money. You paid for it. If you don't take this into account, you can find what the cost per plate is and use a percentage based on that number, but that is really only half the story.

Tristan B. Jones

To make it simple, let's use an example. Let's say you own a restaurant that only sells steak. I don't mean many steaks plural; I mean one kind of steak, on a plate, no seasonings, nothing. Let us put aside things like yields, side dishes, extra items, and salt. We are just talking about pre-packaged ready to go steaks. You are a new restaurant, and you will open your doors in November.

Each steak you order costs you five dollars. You sell each steak for ten dollars, giving you a fifty percent food cost. Simple enough right? Well let's say you order one hundred steaks for the month of November at five dollars per piece, so you spent five hundred dollars. Well, at the end of the month, you realize you only sold seventy of those steaks. The issue is, you paid five hundred dollars, right? And you made three hundred fifty dollars right? Well, what is your food cost? The basic numbers in this situation look like this.

> Steaks in Beginning Inventory: 0
> Number of Steaks Purchased: 100
> Money Spent (MS) on Steak: $500
> Projected Gross Profit: $1000
> Projected Net Profit: $500

KITCHEN FINANCIALS

Amount Sold (AS): 70
Steaks in Ending Inventory (EI): 30
Actual Gross Profit: $700
Actual Net Profit: $200

You see, the net profit is not simply based on what you sold; it is based on what you paid for as a whole. When working out the actual food cost for a month, an easy way to look at it is imagine throwing away the extra thirty steaks. At this point, you need to see what you *actually* paid for those seventy steaks.

This is also why a weekly rotating menu can be very dangerous. If you put say buffalo chicken on the menu one week, and change it next week, but you still have half a gallon of that sauce, what good are you really doing for your restaurant? I can go on and on about rotational menus, and they can be profitable in certain situations with certain clientele, but I digress for now.

Which goes like this:

500 (MS) / 70 (AS) = 7.14

So you actually spent $7.14 on each steak. This means, your *Actual Food Cost Percentage* is:

Selling Price (SP) = $10.00
Money Spent Per Portion (MSPP) = $7.14
7.14 (CPP) / 10 (SP) = .71
.71x 100 = 71
So your *Actual Food Cost Percentage* is 71%

That is a twenty one percent increase from what your projected food cost was supposed to be. This is one of the main reasons amateur restaurateurs fail. They don't understand that food sitting on a shelf not being used is as good as food you threw away, as far as your actual numbers are concerned. This is why having the smallest amount of inventory possible is the ideal situation for any restaurant.

You see this all the time when new restaurant owners start looking at their books, trying to figure out where their money is going. They know they should be at x percent food cost, but when they look at how much they spent vs. how much they made,

KITCHEN FINANCIALS

the number is drastically different than their projections.

In many cases, this causes owners to panic and start running new specials or drastically changing their menus. They will ditch half of the menu and replace it with new items using new ingredients in an attempt to boost sales. What they don't realize is they are only making their problems exponentially worse by adding to their inventory. Now they have even more food sitting on their shelves not being used so their managed volume is astronomical. When their restaurant finally closes they have enough dried pasta to eat for the next year, because they wanted to change the penne to farfalle, maybe they will take the time to reflect, or buy a book like this. They should have used the penne first, or at the very least run it out with specials.

This same basic principal works on a large scale for all products in house going month to month as well, I just wanted to give an easy example with one item and no inventory to start. To ramp this up to all the dishes and inventory pertaining to food, simply use your Beginning Inventory (BI),

Purchases (P), Ending Inventory (EI), and Total Food Sales (TFS).

As in:

$(BI + P) - EI = x$
$x \:/\: TFS =$ Actual Food Cost

Sub COG's or Cost of Goods Sold

Generally, when you are talking about COG's for a restaurant, you are looking at all purchased items vs total sales to a customer. This involves your drinks, paper, chemicals etc. This same formula will help you work out your COGs, you just add in your other items, not just food.

Make sure you take into account the free items such as bread or an amuse bouche as well, or your numbers will be off in the end. Generally, I like to put set a standard price for these items, as costing the amount used each day is possible, but not really a viable solution. Just get an average of the cost these items take, and add a small percentage onto that to be safe.

KITCHEN FINANCIALS

Other Expenses

Many times, when discussing costs for a kitchen, people will add all expenses together to try to work out what they are spending. Do not take this route. This is only a reasonable number to look at if you want to know your COG's, as mentioned before.

All items that are not food should have their expenses worked out separately. This is extremely important to your business as you need to be able to track where your money is going. I suggest breaking them up into paper, chemical, laundry, and other.

Paper

When I say paper, I don't mean just paper. This is just another in a long list of industry terms used to lump multiple things together. Your paper will include things like to-go boxes, paper towels, gloves, paper/foam/plastic cups, and straws. Some of these might be taken care of by the front of the house, but some most certainly will not, and for the most part, the chef or kitchen manager deals with these as he/she does most of the ordering.

People opening restaurants don't ordinarily know how much these products cost. Paper products can slowly eat away at your profits if not kept in check.

Depending on what kind of business you run, the amount and kind of products you need will vary. You will always have your standard Items like gloves and paper towels, but your take-away containers will change. You certainly wouldn't want to spend three hundred dollars on a meal, and when you ask for something to go, it comes in the same box as your local burger joint. If you are making upscale cuisine, I suggest higher quality products. These are much more expensive of course, but you need to keep you perceived value in check.

In recent years, it has become more and more important to ensure all disposable products are eco-friendly. This is another way your cost can become ridiculously high, so you might need to find a company other than your broadliner to supply your needs.

KITCHEN FINANCIALS

Some other miscellaneous items I choose to put in the paper category are things such as, birthday celebration supplies, (sparklers, candles, etc.), bibs for babies, wet naps, twist ties, take away bags, and things of this nature. Not all will apply to you, but these are the kinds of things I include in my paper costs.

Chemicals

You will have to order chemicals for your restaurant and many of them are extremely expensive. Some dishwashers for example can use containers of detergent that can be up to one hundred and twenty dollars for one. In an average restaurant you can go through one of these containers every two days. The money can start to disappear with only essentials needed to operate your establishment.

What you are willing to spend on chemicals is always at odds with your other expenses. Obviously, you would like to spend the bare minimum, but it's never that easy. Here is an example.

Let's say you have a large flat top. This needs to be cleaned every night. There are a couple methods to clean a flat top, but the most common is with a grill brick, some oil, and elbow grease. To properly clean a grill with this method, it takes on average between ten and thirty minutes. If your staff is on overtime from ten dollars and hour to fifteen dollars an hour, you could save money with the right chemicals. If the elbow grease method turns out to be thirty minutes at seven dollars and fifty cents a day, times thirty, that's two hundred and twenty five dollars a month.

With the right chemical however, you can get your cleaning time down to five minutes. There are portion packages with flat top cleaner that turn your black surface sparkly and silver with almost no effort. Many restaurants don't utilize these products because of their price points, but you as a manager need to look at the pros and cons of these decisions, as it's all based on your establishment.

What you actually need to keep on hand is relative to your countries laws. Unfortunately, there is no list of perfect chemicals I can give you. In my kitchens, I like to have; sanitizer, a general cleaning product, (there is a really good orange one in the states), a degreaser, a floor cleaning product, and whatever is necessary for your dish area.

    Luckily, you don't need to make all of these decisions without help. Depending on what company you either buy or lease your dish machine through, you might be able to get chemicals from them. Almost all broadliners carry what is necessary, but not always what is best, or at the best price. So again, make sure you do your due diligence.

Labor Cost

Labor is a huge expense when running a restaurant. As mentioned before, you are a manufacturer as well as a retail business, so you have to be able to take wholesale products purchased and manufacture them into a product you can sell.

Labor cost can kill your net profits just as fast as food cost. To look at the most effective strategy for your restaurant, you need to understand all the factors that go into deciding how to go about it. How many stations do you have in your kitchen? What are your hours/meals you will be open for? What is the level of complexity of your dishes? These aspects will drive your schedule. Dish is pretty straight forward, so we will focus on cooks.

So let's look at what needs to be accomplished on any given shift as it pertains to getting food to the pass. We have looked at stations within the brigade system, and you need to think in terms of the output of each station while considering your schedule. You may own a diner that only

KITCHEN FINANCIALS

needs one cook. You might have a large operation needing ten or twenty cooks on the line at all times. Either way, you need to start your scheduling with stations. Most restaurants of average size utilize the same set up.

    The problem with trying to nail down specifics is the whole station set up depends on the menu. Let's say you have an average American restaurant. Odds are, for a restaurant of average size you will need one person on sauté, doing pasta's and side dishes. He/she will be throwing veggies in a pan for the side with a steak or mixing cream and cheddar in a pan with precooked pasta for mac and cheese. One person on the fry station as your average American joint has a large number of fried item, chicken wings, fries, mozzarella sticks, etc. Next, you will have someone working the cold station. Salads, desserts, sides of cold sauces and the like will be his game. Some lower end places even have the wait staff plate premade desserts, however I advise against this system. In some instances you might also need a grill man, for all the burgers and steaks. That is really all you need. However, do you even have a grill? Are you using a flat top more than an actual grill? Do you need a separate pastry section? Let's try another one.

So Italian is your game. You will have your sauté guy pumping out all of your pasta and fried items. He will be equipped with some gas or induction burners and a fryer. You don't need a fry guy as Italian food doesn't have as many fried items. Working with him you will need someone for meats and any other hot sides, starters and mains. He would be working an oven and a flat top, with a few burners or a small French top for sauces and such. He would prepare things like your fish mains and pork belly starter. You will of course need your cold station for all of the aforementioned reasons. And finally your pastry depends on how you prepare them for service and how nice of a place it is.

I did not mention an expediter, as I could drone on about different set ups, labor cost based on equipment, size, and more. For labor the main focus is to know how your menu is produced and how many people it takes to produce it for your restaurant's size and level of cuisine.

The key here is to use the least amount of money out of your budget to

KITCHEN FINANCIALS

accomplish what you need to get done. Whatever system you start with might end up changing slightly based on your sales, but you need to have a good idea of what will be needed before you open. So how do you keep you labor costs down? Well there are a few ways.

Hourly vs salary

One of the first things I was told when I started culinary school was, and I quote, "Never accept a salary position, they'll work you like a dog." This is true. I have held multiple salaried positions, and with the exception of one, I practically lived at the restaurant. This is an owners dream. I actually calculated how much I would be making an hour at one of these establishments, and it came out to a little over two dollars an hour. This is the a great way to keep labor down, but you can only maintain a system like this if you are one of the top restaurants in your area and young cooks are willing to take horrible pay just for the experience.

This won't work in all countries however. I believe in the states it is the fifty hour mark that you should get compensation for overtime regardless of pay structure. I've never seen this actually amount to anything in our industry, but one of your employees could very well try and have you tied up in litigation for the next year. Generally, your chef and sous chef will be on salary, but your cooks will be hourly. Again, depending on where you live.

Cooks on hourly can be a blessing and a curse. It is nice to be able to send someone home if you are not busy, but this leads to others on the job feeling like they are getting the shaft. Generally speaking, if you are pulling this trick to keep costs down, you are already in trouble.

Cutting prep time

A lot of your restaurants labor cost will go to actually preparing the food before service. You will need to cut your garnish, portion out steaks, set up your stations, and make your sauces. Prep time is necessary regardless of your business, and there are ways to reduce the amount of time necessary for this endeavor.

KITCHEN FINANCIALS

Proper training is your first line of defense. A properly trained employee will be able to run circles around a new guy simply because what he is doing has become second nature. You have to be careful about what you ask an employee to do quickly, as this could lead to injury. Using a knife to slice vegetables quickly, for example, is not something you can teach. You can only show the employee the proper method of say, how to slice an onion, and speed will come later. You can, however, show the employee where the onions are two or three times during training so he/she won't forget where they are.

Proper hiring practices can help as well. I went over hiring practices in the first book of this series, and they will help immensely in many aspects of the kitchen, including keeping costs down. A well-seasoned line cook will bring speed and efficiency to any kitchen position. The less time it takes to execute a task, the more money you will save on labor for that hourly employee.

This brings us to the obvious, pre-prepared or pre-packaged foods. Ordering products you don't need to manufacture into something else will save a lot of money. What needs to be taken into account is quality. If all the burger joints around you are using the same company to order pre-made french fries, will your restaurant stand out using the same product? Probably not, but are your fries a selling point? If your specialty is making the best reuben sandwich in the state, that is what your customers are there for. Could homemade fries help sales? Of course they can. But you would need to order in whole potatoes, cut them either by hand or with a machine, par cook them, and freeze, generally. You can skip the freezing part, but the fact remains.

How many hours of labor are you willing to dump into a product that you sell for one dollar? It all depends on how many you sell and how long it takes to produce, but generally speaking things like fries are better to just order in.

Do not, however, take this too far. Restaurants do this all the time and you can see it in their product. If you are selling fish and chips and you order premade frozen fish sticks, I doubt you will be in business long. You need to carefully consider each menu item, and if you are considering ordering a

KITCHEN FINANCIALS

pre-made product, you need to execute rigorous quality control tests. You need to be able to put your home-made product next to the pre-made, and have nine out of ten people confirm that the pre-manufactured product is better. We have all been to restaurants that everything on the menu is ordered in, and I doubt anyone out there has fond memories of such an establishment.

Cutting your prep time can lead to big savings in the long run, and should be looked into. If you have five staff at ten dollars and hour, you can cut one hour off that and save fifty dollars a day, or fifteen hundred dollars a month. Make sure you pay attention to who is on the clock and when.

So what is my favorite system? Well, salary. Let's look at my preferred method.

My favorite system

So let's look at how I like to set up my kitchens. We will use a restaurant that is only open for lunch and dinner. For this example let's say you open at eleven a.m. and close at eleven p.m. You have two options. Either you have two shifts a day, or one. Regardless, you will need someone there between seven and ten a.m. depending on the menu. The question is, do you have a second shift start in the afternoon? Personally, I prefer one person to work the entire shift. Hold on now, I know what you're thinking, 'but wouldn't that mean someone will be there fourteen to seventeen hours a day?' Yes, it does. Do that five days in a week you will end up around eighty-five hours a week, which will kill you in overtime.

The way this system works is you do those shifts five days in one week, say Monday Tuesday, then again on Friday, Saturday, and Sunday. It is brutal, but the next week your employee trades off with the other person that works their station, so he/she will only work two days in that week. What you end up with is having half of the month off. Even though the hours are brutal on long weeks, only having to work half of the year can be very enticing.

This, however, is not the most beautiful part of this system. With this in place, you only need two people per station. So if your restaurant has grill, sauté, cold, and pastry, you only need eight good cooks to work your line. This will save a lot of headache when it comes to hiring and things

KITCHEN FINANCIALS

like petty disputes. If there is a problem with the station, i.e. it wasn't cleaned properly or a sauce wasn't made correctly, you know exactly who is responsible.

In Europe, it is fairly commonplace. Your salary is based on an agreed upon number, lest say fifteen hundred per month. If you work sixteen days that month, you get an extra hundred for that day. I know what you are thinking, 'What about time and a half'.

I'm not saying this will work in every country around the world, a lot of countries simply will not allow this without a huge amount of compensation. I'm simply saying this is my favorite. Now let's look at the alternative.

With the same opening hours, if you have two shifts per day, you now have sixteen staff members to keep up with, four for each station. This makes your job as a hiring manager and trainer much more difficult. Throw in the turnover rate, and let the fun begin.

Tristan B. Jones

Menu balance

Finally, something that is of upmost importance is the proper balancing of a menu. What does this mean exactly? Well unless you only serve one product the cost on each item will be different. Your order of fries will obviously not have the same cost as your sandwich.

If an order of fries costs you twenty cents to make, and you sell it for one dollar, you have a food cost of twenty percent. If you make a sandwich for one dollar and sell it for ten dollars, you have a ten percent food cost. What then is your food cost for your two item menu? Fifteen percent, that is correct. This is not patronization, I'm simply putting things in the simplest terms.

So how does this relate to balancing your menu?

You will always want to maintain a certain food cost percentage for the entire menu. Generally speaking this number will depend on the type of food and services. As an example, many fine dining restaurants will have a much higher food cost percentage

KITCHEN FINANCIALS

because they make that money back with wine. On the other hand, if you sell hamburgers, no one is buying a three hundred dollar bottle to go with their meal.

The average restaurant will be trying to hit a food percentage mark around thirty three percent. If you only sling hamburgers and fries or sandwiches, you can shoot for twenty-eight. Most fast food chains are even lower, but when you have the corporate might to get tax cuts, you have more options than any normal business. Finer restaurants can go as high as forty, sometimes more, but this is getting into territory that is very rare.

As an example, let's look at a normal restaurant, they serve steaks, some seafood, pasta, salads, etc., and keep it simple. Their menu may look like this:

>   Starters
>   Shrimp Skewers- $9.99
>   Pork Belly- $7.99
>   Duck Croquettes- $6.99
>
>   Salads
>   Caeser Salad: $8.99
>   House Salad: $6.99

Mains
Filet with Asparagus- $24.99
Lobster with Kohlrabi- $32.99
AOP Pasta- $12.99
Cajun Chicken with Hominy- $15.99
Duck with Raspberry- $19.99

Dessert
Fried Banana with Caramel- $6.99
Spicy Chocolate Mousse- $9.99

How does this place make money? Most would look at the lobster and filet and immediately assume these are the money makers. This is actually the opposite of reality. That lobster is expensive, and so is the steak. They are probably running around forty five to fifty percent food cost on these items. Your restaurant will fail with these numbers, so where does the money come from and how do we balance it?

Well, look at the salads. They are simple and probably only cost about a dollar to produce, so they are going to be somewhere in the teens as far as percentage is concerned. The starters follow the same basic principal, as you can use a very small portion of a protein, and still maintain a very high perceptual value.

KITCHEN FINANCIALS

A basic plate of AOP costs less than a dollar to produce, so you are looking at around nine percent food cost. This is the reason pastas are such a mainstay at a lot of restaurants. They are filling, delicious, and most of all, cheap.

After you average all of these different items together, you will hit your butter zone. This is all menu balancing boils down to. Take a hit on some items, and make your money elsewhere.

This is why balancing a menu is essential. You need to keep your food cost percentage at a reasonable level, but no one will want to pay ninety dollars for a steak, unless you are in a nice establishment where that is expected.

You do still need to pay very close attention to your numbers. If you only sell steaks for a whole month, you could be losing money hand over fist. Luckily, most people will order either the lowest cost main course or something mid-range. It is rare that only the high priced items will be the ones to sell, but it is something to look out for. If your lower cost items are not getting ordered, you either have to increase the cost of your expensive items, which can irritate repeat customers, or you can take another look at your lower cost items. Maybe no one in your area knows what AOP is, and that's the main reason it isn't selling. Maybe the description on the menu isn't appealing enough. As a relatively new restaurant, maybe your clientele is looking for a nicer dining experience and you should think about re-working your concept. The bottom line is, pay attention.

KITCHEN FINANCIALS

Profit Bombs

I am aware that most of this book has been gloomy. It seems there is so much that goes into maintaining a profitable kitchen it can get discouraging. So let's look at what you can do to make some easy money. I call these profit bombs.

These 'profit bombs' are simple things you can do to bring more money into your kitchen. They in no way are put in place to substitute proper financial management of your kitchen, they are just a way to bring in some extra cash, and maybe give you a glimmer of hope after a long day of crunching numbers.

We discussed how things like pastas on the menu are a great way to balance an overall food cost percentage, but don't forget, fifty cents is fifty cents, especially when it hits your bottom line. Things like sides of sauces, extra sauces, menu modifications, special orders, and charging for to go containers can bring in that little bit of extra cash.

Tristan B. Jones

Listen, you don't want to charge for all of these things, especially not all at once in the same restaurant. Your customers will begin to feel cheated, like you are trying to nickel and dime them out of things that are generally free. You should not, however, be intimidated by charging for some things that cost you money.

If you own a pizza/calzone restaurant and half the tables order an extra side of marinara, at two ounces a pop times one hundred and thirty covers, that's a gallon of sauce! You're darn straight you need to charge for that. If you buy eco-friendly to-go containers at seventy five cents a piece, when you could get them for five cents a piece, maybe you should charge for them.

What you can and cannot charge for depends on the same basic principles as a lot of things in this book, like what country you are in and the restaurant culture there. For example, when I went to a fast food place here in Europe for the first time, (I won't name names but they sell burgers), I was shocked when they charged me twenty five cents for a ketchup package. There would be riots in America over such and outrage! But that's just how it is.

KITCHEN FINANCIALS

So when you are looking at charging someone for something, especially if it is not on the menu, be careful. The last thing you want is an irate customer screaming at a waitress over a side of ranch. Some things, like the eco-friendly to go containers are an easy sell, but some may cause emotional reactions in your customers. Going to other establishments with similar concepts around you can help you get a firm grasp on what is deemed acceptable in your area.

When considering what you can and cannot charge for, just remember this basic rule; only charge for what you feel is acceptable. If you would be angry at another restaurant for charging for that item, your customers will be too.

In Summation

Running a profitable kitchen has so many factors to look at there is almost never an easy answer for any one problem. You need to have comprehensive view of the entire operation before you try to solve a problem. You might end up looking at only one factor of the issue when there are ten factors at play.

The easiest way to get a good idea of what needs to be addressed is looking at everything as if it were money. Too many new restaurateurs slough off small costs as insignificant; however these are the backbone of your business. Every drop of oil or ounce of sauce is what comprises most of the money in your restaurant so don't take them for granted.

As always I suggest hiring a professional chef to help guide you if you are either new to the industry, or are trying to improve your business. Some reading this might already be on a downward slope trying to survive and can't afford one, and that's ok. That is why I am writing this series and

KITCHEN FINANCIALS

keeping the cost of these books low. I am here to help. If you are ever in a situation you don't know how to fix, and need some help, you are always welcome to contact me.

    Good luck my friends, and stay vigilant.

Tristan B. Jones

KITCHEN FINANCIALS

For further information I am available for consultation at

Chef.tristan.jones@gmail.com

Tristan B. Jones

KITCHEN FINANCIALS

www.ingramcontent.com/pod-product-compliance
Lightning Source LLC
Chambersburg PA
CBHW020444220526
45464CB00002B/845